Repairs

A Breakthrough Book
No. 32

REPAIRS

Poems by
G. E. Murray

University of Missouri Press
Columbia & London
1979

University of Missouri Press, Columbia, Missouri 65211
Library of Congress Catalog Card Number 79–5379
Printed and bound in the United States of America

Library of Congress Cataloging in Publication Data

Murray, G E   1945-
Repairs.

(A Breakthrough book ; book 32)
I.   Title.
PS3563.U768R4   811'.5'4   79-5379
ISBN 0-8262-0290-X

For My Mother and Father,
And for Theirs, and Again Theirs

The Devins Award for Poetry

Repairs is the 1979 winner of the Devins Award for Poetry, an annual award originally made possible by the generosity of Dr. and Mrs. Edward A. Devins of Kansas City, Missouri. Dr. Devins was President of the Kansas City Jewish Community Center and a patron of the Center's American Poets Series. Upon the death of Dr. Edward Devins in 1974, his son, Dr. George Devins, acted to continue the Award.

Nomination for the Award is made by the University of Missouri Press from those poetry manuscripts selected by the Press for publication in a given year.

Contents

Holding Fast, 9

Part One: Reducing the Herd

Part Two: Light Travels, Impassable Roads

Holding Fast

To hell with flowers
and sentimental train rides.

I prefer to travel alone,
by knee, like a gardener,
thankful for weeds.

Part One

Reducing the Herd

Reducing the Herd

Beyond the customary methods—
a pistol to the head,
arsenic in drinking troughs,
throats slit like melons—

there are questions of the pit,
its capacity and width,
who turns the soft earth open

against the low of half-knowing calves?

I prefer thinning the herd
by breed, age, nature of disease.
Young Jerseys

first, the prod-proof ones,
given to bewilderment
and double scoops of feed.

Certain Holsteins next,
the strays, the weaklings,
laying low
in patchwork fields.

Then those Herefords,
crossbred into dreaminess . . .

All losers at market,
all dumped from hoppers,
their necks ripe with fear,
their confusion high as the sun.

    *   *   *

Call it slaughter,
call it necessity.

We're sore from the trouble.

Tired of shooting
daylong until dark,

I watch those chosen
drop hard into carcass.

None of us likes it much.
To right the selection,
bury the kill

before our children
spot a favorite
twitching in the trench—

that's the trick!

*   *   *

We rock down the day's sun
in armchairs of privilege.

In the loins of what we keep
new strains of nuisance
root like weeds.

We accept this,
and clean our guns regular.

I sit content with evening's rest
under a warm lampshade,
headlines unread in my lap,
twilight turning down the fields
like a great feather bed

as our children lope off
after supper.

In a hardwood barn
the good beef grazes
on dark obedience,
sensing us.

Camped in old ways,
our hands washed
daily in milk,

we lie back to snore
and remember nothing.

American Cheese

She was made from scratch in Wisconsin,
Slowly at first, given to disguises
As a child, a figure swept
By sunshine toward the free fall
Terror in her heart. A declension of circles,
She grew round and firm and ready,
A processed miracle,
Sealed in wax of nervous gestures,
Exported to Chicago as a necessary foodstuff—
Old prairie fiction.
When she turned the wind's
Hard corner, aging decades in days,
She announced, during a daylight attack
Of logic, straight up and down
Like an exclamation point, she was her own
Worst obsession, the failed product
Of a putty knife. Years later,
Crazy on Clark Street, her one stocking
Rolled below the snow line
Of an ankle swollen with city winters,
She becomes available
As litter, blown around the trainless
Midnight of Union Station, talking
A blue streak to the terminal darkness.
In the midlands, there is no telling
The stories of the dead.

The Hungarian Night

From trees fall shavings of her darkest enthusiasms.
Her face that rivets breezes, the chilling soil
Of our riverside walk, go warm to furnished anterooms

Of dear Budapest. We share a borrowed Cuban cigar,
Railway stories, a coin to rent two hours of heat.
Look at her green stockings hung almost unremembered,

Slipping from chairback to floor, like eels.
Night turns wet, and pronouncements of tea leaves
Govern her officious dealings with the planet.

Night is a worm in the heart, she says, an ancient worm
Eating granite. Soot drops from nowhere, the sky.
There's a battle scene we recognize carved on the bedboard.

Above attics in the musty capital, smokestacks huddle
Like brown monkeys. Someone dies crying in this place.
Someone opens to blood storm and heresy. Sirens

Mired in alleys say it's so. Downstairs a café stinks
Of cabbage and pepper soup, stays lit by lavender neon.
We can believe the faded meanings of tapestry

And that moment of pilgrimage now, the skull bone
Buzzing empty, without ambition or reluctance.
Next door a man wheezes and sputters, healing from
Dreams of absinthe, white suits, and slow ceiling fans.

The Poem Hangs Its Hat

It fits the hammock
like a pouch of slag . . .

Still inside the park,
the poem is on vacation.
It tells the flag
how to fake a breeze,
how the cripple weaves
a formula for grace.

It speaks of skyrockets.
It picnics alone.
It buys used opera tickets.

But get the poem drunk!
Let it hunt
for the back of its brain.
It will sweat on the streetcar.
It will pay its own fare.
Ah, the poem begins to moan . . .

Night Crawlers

"In the countryside the enemy almost
completely controls the night."

—Robert McNamara, *The Pentagon Papers*

We lie here worming holes
Through the lips of the night.

When the swamps whistle dark
With hunger, we slip into fields
On sponge paws, mending chunks
Of country with flesh and terror . . .

Through the high wet grasses
And tunnels that hatch
Into hives of fury, we smash
At the marble eye of our other—

The enemy. We are absent now:
The day passes; crickets wake.
Across the waste of paper years,
Wars blend like seasons. Ignorance

Or venom, we are blessed and believe
Just the same. In these iron hours,
Tokens of death infect the night,
So perfectly dense with jasmine.

And again our long muscles
Are lying tense as a code . . .
It is the sky of another night:
Blood will collect in puddles.

Listen now, we start our crawling . . .
Defend yourself against the stars!

Invasion of the Muses

We'll never do it with bullets alone,
And this steady menace has grown
Immune to napalm, the common cold,

Even elaborate traps of electric death.
Once, when we thought we isolated
The danger, we took pains to airlift

The lot of them south to Antarctica.
They wouldn't freeze. They won't leave.
Instead they proliferate, infiltrate

Our young like acne, slithering from
Everywhere to possess the skies of our life.
We have repelled this fright too long.

New surefire defenses will be available soon.

Indian Tricks

Old totems
full of aches
mark the interstate
I take to Ponca City:

clever ambush.

*   *   *

In the desert at noon,
an old Navajo
filling with cloudburst,
rocks in the shade
of a single gas pump.

*   *   *

A game of darts
over morning beers

in Ponca City's
Gallery Café.

A browned kid
comes in to rattle

a Coke machine,
sell watches.

No drink, no takers.
Disgusted, he fingers

a sweaty dart
and whips it

over rows of bottles
at the cheap print

of Custer frozen
in his "Last Stand."

Thwack!
Silence applauds

the new arrow
in Yellow Hair's hat.

    *   *   *

Minus the moccasins,
elkskin shirts,
ceremonies of speech,
they are nothing.

When they rub
against trees,
they burn away:

smokeless industries.

    *   *   *

They were nothing.
There is proof.

I photograph
two Indians
talking.

Weeks later,
in the darkroom,
only their voices
develop.

The Chocolate Infection

Days of the ferret, a sweet fever.
Someone is walking through the sun
With my tongue on a leash.

Say "Ahhh." Thank goodness,
It's not diabetes or the Bolivian Rot.

This morning I am a cross
Between lefthandedness
And pointblank rage.

The sun leaks like soft ice.
The infection deepens . . .

My eyes dissolve
In a closet of heat.
I become 4,000
Yellow flowers, chirruping.

O the cliché of a trek into the bowels of China.
O the night that zings like a harpsichord factory!
O gorgeous sun limping in the frozen dusk.
O candy wrappers stacked like bricks!

Snow growls on my roof.
The infection deepens . . .

A day on fire
Placing real rabbits
Where my mouth should be.

I am several kinds of tigers.
I am a confectionary treat.

This fever fills my sleeves
With pearls of honey drops.
Am I too strange to bleed?

I'm behind myself
With a knife and fork,
Revolving on a skewer.

I am wild with grief
As greasy children
Reach deep into my fever
To scoop out their revenge
In double-dips . . .

Come off it, kids.
Next week, I'll be raining
On the iron road to Malta
And perfect health, melting
Like sugar in the mouth of the Orinoco.

The Dirt Prescriptions

Keeping it clean
here on this page immaculate
as a blood oath,

we know doses of premium dirt,
alluvial silt
and tear-moistened

clay proper
can be kinder to us
than health

or the anonymous machinery
of skies
blue as acetylene.

      *   *   *

Naming the dirt
of beggars and sunbathers,
of missionaries

and tufted armchairs,
we make sacred
the fictions of living with dirt.

      *   *   *

Imagine the many crimes of dirt
during harvest,

the resulting sadnesses
of carpets.

Imagine dust that rolls
like longboats

at mooring, awaiting
new clarification

on the meanings of dirt:
our sources, our scatterings.

*   *   *

The spotless night
goes on being night,

while light
pursues a lyric

at the open window. Consider
all else as us:

temporary movements,
predestined dirts.

*   *   *

Inherit the patience
of dirt. Thrive silently.

It's that complex.

What the Toads Were Told in Paradise

I'm heating a stone in the local jungle;
It becomes an ax on this rock fire.
Blind as lice, the toads are watching
My poems roast like almonds. I am bad
At authority, bad at whipping large dogs,

So I twist at the woods with my ax and stop
The toads in their blood. I hack
At bellies that balloon like goiters.
I chew on tendons, nipping their sweetness.

The surprise of the ax!
There is fungus black as an ox
Tongue on the ground. It swells like tetanus
In a dripping wound. I have come to this—
Repairing myself with the musk of toads.

I have nearly broken through to their deaths
In Paradise: the toads are towering
Like breath in winter. They are whispering
In the pulp of this paper—the wind in a pyx:

"His ax is a poem, and he leaps like toads,
Waiting for the poke of God's fat finger."

Monologue with a Mackinaw

These December latitudes, the tattered rags of snow
    still spread on the ground like oily doves
In flight, whole armies of wind unglued in my jacket,
    slice Vermont into strips of panfried liver.
I end peeling away leaves of myself like lettuce, until
    just the flavor is left from this feast
Of rivers and forest breath, cold as birch on white sky.
    The knapsack at hand is a worthless tonic;
Folk songs and fires bore the life out of decent hills.
    I will write home tomorrow. I will say
The splendor of New England is contagious as a club foot;
    its winter shades starker than even Kandinsky
Could fathom—virgin pinks, sunken suns, the light smack
    of fate and tired soil. There is singing
Inside maple, the wild voice of syrup. Now I understand
    why friends cherish good business sense,
Opportunity, the animal power of a country sedan.
    I dispatch my teenage spirit to Boston,
Where debates glisten like the back of a raspberry picker,
    and air is fat. Crimes against pine trees
Are judged in the available dark: guitar laughter, solemn
    hikes, Boy Scout troops lifting their legs
High on command, like Noh dancers troubled by bugs.
    Nights here stretch forward. The tonsils
Of spring are impossible to find by the only log fire
    in miles. When it burns, you can touch
Whatever comes next. I wore the wigs of marriage badly.
    Scattered returns are hard to collect.

Losing Altitude

I gray and become
one on the move,
ferocious, lovable,
useful as a poker chip.
I wonder about flying
over Dakota's snow,
a serial number & shadow.
Keeping faith
with a magazine
and second Scotch,
I relax eastward
like a cash register
closed out for the day.
Far ahead, fired hard
by sleep's luscious fuel,
I fix on how
tall women talking
will fill the bars
in Chicago tonight
like electricity;
how home is
a lakefront of bandits
bootlegging spirit.
I grow comfortable
in my suit. I fit
this swift nest.
The engine jumps
like a dental patient.
My drink spills
into a flannel stain,
a birthmark spreading
larger than the century
I descend from quickly.

Specimens of Spring

Humor and footing improve.

The storied paralysis of water finally retreats,
Pleasing even fish.

Along Avenue C, a breakfast league of women
Go shopping pushcarts
In fuzzy slippers, flowered housecoats,

Eternally seeding
The botanies of spring.

And in Saint-Tropez, diamonds
And the prevailing radiance of cocktail onions

Sparkle intensely as beauty parlor intrigues.

There are mice in the kitchen again,
And in blood's fantasy,
A new blueing. Off Hatteras,

Wings of cloud fan like tobacco leaves,
Then parade away like Shriners,

While ocean breakers boom ancient operas at rock.

Nowhere does dreaming muster so,
Or leap to cleave
Longing and winterkill

From the day that first tightropes
Among groves of oleander and hawkweed.

Spiraling under this season's needle,

A music of design
Freshens on its turntable.

If valleys were living choirs
Once more, sacrosanct and believing,

All newborn things would lower,
Listen hard,

And early on, survey echoes

Of boot thump, paw and cane, the crusty hooves
Of a blind horse led stumbling to plow

Its own grave, a beginning.

Love in Its Hearse

As with a dusty-rose colored morning that shaved too close,
August's in a mood, a lather of heat. Under a monk's hood
Of composure, people sizzle in place like steaks
Turned medium-rare. Rag awnings and cheap foliage
Endure, inevitable as sage brush dancing hot
To saxophone winds. Daylight when sky drowses,
There's a canvas of landscape poised after rain,
The rustle of fowl in a forest clearing where
No fowl exist. Later then, someone's slim blond daughter
Goes horsebacking in the high pines, neither
Alone nor distant, but a disciple of love. Elsewhere,
Say, north-northeast, sea gulls have come
And gone already, while pale men in slickers
Breakfast on kippers and salted eggs.
So it's sunshine off the hushed eucalyptus
That reminds of Morocco, even Caracas, those leotards
Of vision cut from the hides of fitful sleep. Variously,
Like sands at migration, we embark
Instantly, without dream or token destination.
Ah, how certain the wind veers in all directions now,
As if a loved one. Near the scuttled coast in late summer,
One star huddles like a fugitive among marshy vapors.
It's a dying dark, volunteer dark, island
Darkness that grips like a grape on its seed.
It was the sound of this darkness that tore like a muscle.
In August, here or anywhere, a chorus of love's lean memories
Delivered into coarse riddle, a persuasion
Against design, an open blouse, the blush
Of disappointment. The self-possessed repair with teasings,
Their eyes given to fits of exhaustion, eyes
Thrashing for love, reconstituted love. This proves
Serious play. And desire becomes an isolation. Often,
In the simmering of summer's night, we maneuver
In pairs, comparing notes on anatomy, spread-eagled
Below sealed French windows, on manicured lawns
Of adjacent estates of mind, nervous and secretive as caretakers.
We moonlight in the oil-lamp light of a tar-paper moon.
Night alone seems voluptuous enough. Maple trees
In a mist will also suffice, containing sweet liquid,
Releasing much more, this porridge of feeling, this tender ooze.

Somewhere, lightning drums the horizon like a rolling pin.
In time, the heated sky will clarify butter.
What lays under, what flows toward the far shore is
What's meant by human music—chic,
So virtuous, a long and complex score in the unmaking.

Everything knows its own untold story: The hair suddenly
Depilated, birds starving in a future snow,
The crisis of spinal columns set marching to strains from
Love's accordion. Voila! Conversely, summer thunder
Purifies sea salt, shaken from the cold palm
Of history. This side of death the features of twilight
Imitate the palpable dream of love
Mounted like an engine, secure in its workings
And thankful for the work. We can lay track
When we know how we are going, whether to haunt
Gray backwaters in a raincoat's slouch, or darken like beans
Trapped in a meditation of sun. There's
Mystery in the dedicated twitterings
Of anonymous birds, in the bell-moan of a freighter
As it proceeds through a fog bank, becoming fog.
But intrigue we abort, denigrate as a posture
Assumed by a figure shadowboxing room to vacant room
In an old wooden building. Occasionally, pausing
To peer out—perhaps sight a daughter riding the high pines—
The figure betrays itself as an honorable illusion.
This is one way to calibrate the shapes of love
Painlessly, with a sense of event and compensation.
Thus, again it's believed that weather hangs like a drape,
And behind it, a couple quietly talking with their hands
And feet, musing small differences, in early afternoon.
They prefer converging pauses, love among strangers,
Negotiable bonds. It's often the same on a speeding train
As in a musty parlor occupied only by denials of light.
Even when tedium fades dead away, it's likely we yearn
For sunrise and the accumulation of flowers.
Only the churning beauty of it all—
Self's originality—turns remote and unfixable
As our lucky stars. In disguises of surveillance,

Planned advances, we are cut from love's modern cloths—
Velours and worn corduroy, our bloodied pajamas.
It's shooting season, a time to wear red, go hunting
Dust and whispers, a love that cures ham. And higher up,
The wind stalls, warm and empty-handed, its engines
Ghosting away in the hibernation of a blank sky.
Once more, discussing river life, we turn on our spigots,
Politely pouring air at an outdoor café—our talk
Of paddle-wheelers and wine lists everywhere,
Anticipation of flaming desserts, blind carnival
In the streets, chess games stalemated on the green, two
Or three of us waving adieux to love in its hearse.

Part Two

Light Travels,
Impassable Roads

Somewhere in Boston There's a
Bridge Writing Music

A bridge at my bare feet, imagining music . . .

In its dark mind the bridge
Strains like the nose of a drowning man
To hatch a new cantata,
Baroque as cancer, and nearly conscious
Among the bars without sawdust,
The lamps without gas, a soft laughter.

The bridge works late within the mist's
Delicate steel ear,
Takes notes, revises, and sulks—
An exile in a free-port café.
It forgets how its brain has never lived.
It sings in the shape of its loneliness . . .

And what lugged the pilings here?
Who mends the cracks
That break over Boston like reeds,
Thinner than blindness?

The bridge senses its rhythms
With excitement, a trapper tracking himself
In a fever, farther and farther north,
Calculated, mad, understandable circles,
A music that swirls under my feet and disappears
Like a wader moving into his own shadow.

Gulls in Gloucester Harbor

Small things astonish us. The insolence of toys, a
willful clock. Even famous signatures, if they respond
to our needs as these gulls do. Each morning another
catch of cod goes to auction, the one-eyed filets of
our sadness. And the gulls circle in an irregular
holding pattern. How little fuel their language uses!
Sometimes they appear to be flying outward from a century in
which nothing was born. A sharp rain comes
whipping down the street now, solitary as a wasp. The
small shops close, appearing later on a souvenir
ashtray somewhere in Detroit. Our nets need repair,
as does the obsolete tide that dies in our sleep.
Coastal fog rides in and out like a set of tranquilized
buttocks, a fisherman's last gesture to the memory
of his wife.

Chicago as the Time of Night

to Michael Healy, in Cambridge, Mass.

With Chicago underfoot and spoiling
like a month-old egg, a hair of music
in the city's unkempt dish of butter,
I add this place to my necklace of schemes.
Pure East, pure cream, I'm wrinkled like skin
on a mattress, next to false teeth and rouge . . .
This is just scuttlebutt: on central time,
dying is an irrelevant surprise.
The infinite gray and meager shock of wedding
the midlands hits colder than a left hook.
I'm keeping track of the lost fantastic jazz
and mobs, wearing a castaway fedora . . .
I'm up-country in the good straw to stay.
For now, it's almost atomic, baby.

California Dead

In golden winters one misses them most,
the fabulous dead of California,
baked like bricks
into perpetual tans of the earth's choosing.
I sometimes hear their slight voices,
long gone, rise from the dirt plumbing
in this seaside motel . . .

I think they might come north by mule train,
over some ridge, in the clear of day,
missionaries with tight blue lips,
who would descend like radio signals
to a flock of freeway traffic
roaming in an hour glass. And I think
they would make hay out of flavor straws,
swimmers, set designers, the Sunset Strip,
before drawing close a crucifix of mind.
What antique scabs must line their robes,
what savagery they'd read in junk-car smiles.
It's difficult to watch them naked now,
walking again the plazas of dim instinct,
in search of the one Indian guide
who returned them to this wild territory.

New Orleans, October's First Sunday

The Waking

Colors of soul meander, the morning
Could mean biscuits, corn flakes, chicory
Thick as sea fog, grits. Instinct's string
Yanks you upright to light. For a fee,
You live. Your flat sausage of a body
Fries in bed on the month's first holy day.
Outside, albums of moss open
In absolution of this place, this wail
Of an almost island, dripping garden
Wall and terrace stone. Alone the handrail
Of sunrise, knee-high in sheets, you leave
The horizontal, aching, eager to lead
The life of your poverty, eager to bleed.

Noon Walk

In the beehive daylight of Rue Toulouse,
Shadows hang like Spanish hair, leap
From second-story porches like suicides.
In this high, fluttering brightness,

You walk abandoned and lost as a history
Of Cajun wars, fatigued of eloquence,
But strolling still. Like bluegrass and steely jazz,

The rhythms of your presence are all improvisation,
Marginal and fleeting. For the particulars,
You draw back pink bamboo curtains and stop,
Delivered again to a blur of amusements—
French enamels, long-legged crystal,
A flush of conversation
Extending like a gambler's smooth handshake.

That's an old tuxedo shirt and black tie
You wear religiously, your silks
On stone, caring less. And here, your heart

Dresses as a swamp of affections. In midday
Light, among flora and horsecarts, you
Hazard a tour of yourself, rigging out
Like an embrace, a perishable—

Moving transparently, inexhaustible
As air at a shrimp boil, and moving, you
Become the long afternoon, a shadow forming.

Nightwatch

Weaving home in pieces, the breeze
Tows you south by southeast, wind
Brushing you with its lace hands
Like a girl, a summer curtain.
Banks of fog lift off the coast
In cotton puffs. You rise
To plunge on the deck of gray spaces,
The whale of your own creation.
You comb night's gumbo from your hair.
Moonless, sun-wary,
Two more blocks to mooring,
Your masquerade as a coffin works:
Closed in wood, mouth cut wide,
You shape the new week's first scream.

Tiger on Michigan Avenue

"A tiger does not have to
proclaim his tigritude."
—Wole Soyinka

When this ton of tiger
was dumped at my heel
like a keg of cognac
or fossil fuel, I rode
the slow suds down
Michigan Avenue, past
Bonwit's, toward Saks,
into Peck & Peck and death.

This is pure tiger juice,
I thought, the concentrated
residue of jungle pelts
and aged thunder. Not
just puma dust, filet
of cougar or lion cream,
but tiger juice!,
so real and sweet
in my glutted parts.
I think I spent the day
as a tiger, stalking
the hot scent of hemlines
and popcorn through
a turnstyle crowd. I
heard Chicago thump
like a buried drum. I
set my paws before short,
bewildered shoe clerks. Now
and then, I snarled "blood,"
slid onto the sidewalk,
a dangerous stripped glove.
I hung around manholes;
I knew about traps.
It was lovely as I flung
my tail between small talk
and stool pigeons
in a country of eyes.

And just when my happiness
flashed in the street
like a succulent peacock,
I dreamt of my skin
as lilies, and lost it.
All the swagger and growl,
all the useless grinning—gone.
I scurried through the waste
of shoppers and confetti,
fell apart like a puzzle.
"The tiger is here!
The tiger is here,"
I whispered at the dark,
automatic world, sluggish
and unknown as I sunk
into waves of asphalt,
an embarrassed periscope.

Driving Wheels

I am thinking of Iowa
After Christmas in a roadhouse,

The wind's force, and coffee
Like a driving wheel.

Don't take coffee lightly.
It's a nation builder!

The holy aroma of work
Is ground roasted & bitter, too.

A sprocket for our driving wheels?
The darker the better, eh?

The wind, like coffee, warms
Our smiles. The wind is everything.

Looking across the breast
Plate of pickle-green Iowa.

I think over the clack
Of saucers & wet napkins

Soaking our spills—
A tonic for the smudges

Of Christmas. It is morning
In Des Moines, & still no snow.

"Pass the cream, please . . ."
I feel dark natives

Shucking pods & grinning
Like the smooth, fat blades

Of machetes. Quick as weeds,
The wind pockets our lives,

Our crashing cups & anger.
Outside, the highway sags.

Corn steams in Iowa
Like a day-old pot,

A barnful of *National Geographics*,
A faith in brown beans.

I heal from a flow of coffee
Fresh in my throat,

Swell through the ruins
Of a terrible distance.

These wheels . . .

In Memory of a Coastal November

The wind keelhauling
November again. The facile women
Gathering tweed

Goods on the veranda, watching sloops
Drop out of season.
Block Island,
Kennebunkport, South Bay,

Wherever a solitary tourist slouches
Away unnoticed, faintly waving
Farewell to a sea town's
Bait of water,
Its weathered clapboard.

By afternoon, the usual musics
Play to both sides
Of louvered doors—
Edith Piaf
On Victrola;
Birds sweetening
Rain shortened days.

And there are collars turned against
Gooseflesh, against the idle gazing
In the parlor of a maiden aunt.

All these passages clearing at once
Are called November
As it fades, as a herringbone sky
Settles everywhere,
Over shoreline and pierview,
The shuttered marketplace,
A tear vase.

And the women continue darning
The men into tweed.
And the clapboard, the lapping water,

Still await the advent of small occasion.

Missouri River Poem

Blue gleam of Irish moss
in Baptist Missouri,
curl of light,
triangular
across mad waters,
plankton, skipping stone,
like the vanishing tracks
of fish. Dark machine,
after a hard day
watching you surge and knock
against two shores,
trafficking this summer
into a vast dream
of wheat,
I sit alone, banking
the year's yield
in a fist of water.

The Florida Elegies

To the frog-belly white skins of northern ladies
Suffering sun, to that pageant
Of tropical complaints; a certain light
Gleaming in oil of a dark Cuban eye . . .

I.

Here's the odd company of strangers and weather,
Of lives expectant, mingling like sweat.
Keeping pleasant and regular
In the wake of such intricate heat,
Let's welcome night-wind
Mandolins, swim cleansing
Seas off Key West; observe
The red-blackened skies
Moving over Miami, disease-free.
Let's argue the matter, adjust
The apparatus of being
Like a chaise lounge;
Inventory stories of the poor
Just for practice.
As we kill time
At the flower stall,
At the Natural Juice Booth,
At dogtracks
Of daily illumination,
We confess to arts
Of gardening and profit,
Value leisure days
As if gifts from official acquaintances.

Under our red-and-white-striped cabanas,
In convalescent sun
And receding coconut waters,
Among palmetto fronds
And photographable smiles,
We become fragile as innuendo.
In time, we respond only
To the late afternoon
Clinking of flagpole chains
Sounding dinner.
We are better when
We walk the charter-boat docks
Making notification
Of prize fish and secular games—
Nothing worth remembering
But the usual asides,
Lime vodka flowering
In us, helping negotiate
Exquisite journeys
Between jetty and terrazzo,
As we set half sail
On this dreamboat evening,
Tiring of a song
That never plays long or clearly enough.

II.

Down in Apalachee County
the worst of all
is habitual: pitiless drone

of airboats, formidable
gossip of mangroves.
Miles out on Welfare Island

there are threadbare cattle
playing house
in channel foam; women

working barefoot in a creek;
rain-gray faces
watching all. You know

the coursing of these shoals,
the swamp musk
that directs like a map

of diminishing returns.
Turning dusk,
you catch a scent of dogs

prowling hot in lowland fog,
pursuing night
howls. From a backroom dark

you hear a girl give hard
birth, gasping
like failed refrigeration.

III.

Cancel the season, this holiday trance . . . Having crowded
Once onto some swollen finger of land at the tip
Of continent, in a casket of sun, too dazzled to squander
These generous occasions of reef and sky, we begin
Driving out from the glowing cities.
                              What is it,
Coastal and mournful, we chase? The languor of beds
Unmade, long days of television taken prone, like oxygen;
Gumdrops found between the sheets? Being wiser,
We blaze down A1A, past groves of derelict pickers, remote
Monuments to fruit, saffron buildings lining
The shores of this inlet where we learn to live
Among kitchenettes and empty wire hangers.
                              Such is illusion,
A piping from bamboo flutes, thought strangely housed.
But even when we doze, we hear a slithering of lizards
Herd through night, the busy hands of those who carve
Love on public walls, a caterwauling outside
The dog and cat cemetery. Slack-jawed then, we appear
Completed this night by a promise of blackening waters
No one has ever crossed.

48

A Brief History of Aerial Romance
Over North America

You know stories of the handsome mechanic
Who nonchalantly spins
Into the sputtering kiss
Of a propeller,

Or the navigator who confuses
His reflection
For some guiding light,
Only to soar north alone
Toward permanent midnight,

Or the crashed pilot
Trapped for hours
In wilderness
As a cracked motor
Bubbles into his eyes.

            *   *   *

For all we hear
Our fears obscure the worst
Abuses of sky.

Still you believe we will arrive
By dead reckoning,
Our shuttled dreams intact.

I tell you we have already
Flown over the edge
We always knew was looming there.

Sketch for a Morning in Muncie, Indiana

Forget the time spent mining the rudiments of praise.
Central Indiana is left to the man who fuels his
morning with soft-boiled eggs and the veins in a fat
waitress's legs.

All his aliases are forgotten; he prefers loneliness
to life among some hairs in his comb. Several inches
beneath his skin there are musicians with arthritic
fingers, hordes of accomplished clarinets, twin pianos
like lobster claws, melodies from a soundless culture.
Only the neat, golden fields of Indiana hear them, and
waltz furiously out of step, like a row of pom-pom
girls drunk on the promise of cherry cokes and the
coach's good looks.

Then the countryside traffic begins to form into
clouds of crows, a symphony of his own that he remembers.
The last gulp of juice goes down like premium gasoline.
He rises, fumbles for spare change with the embarrassment
of a virtuoso searching absentmindedly for a missing
suite. I pick up the tip he leaves, and pocket it.

Falling Asleep in Empire, Colorado

I still ride nighthawk
on the pampas of her sleep.

She spins freely,
luminous as a watch hand
ticking toward the intricate

clockworks of morning.

A wind bangs down this valley.
Rustlers hover drunk in the hills.
Night rides herd on the yelps of night.

Roaming the fences
sleep invents,
I double back
for repair
to her bare shoulder.

We have no branding irons
heating in the fire;
no tinhorn's oath
wedged like prayer
in the bunkroll of darkness.

In love, we will be
drovers, breaking camp,
upright in tomorrow's saddle,

dreaming fandango.

Mythmaking on the Merritt Parkway

Aluminum sky. Only November
Leaks into early frost
Like a ruptured jug
Of gas. I'd rather hold
Onto this road with pliers
Than have another face of you
Frisk my heart. Cool hands,
The touch of every moon
Is crucial and incomplete
As a sponge bath. Leaving
A backbone of lights
Behind me, a blinking string
Of pelts in fox country,
I long to slice through
Connecticut's middle, marbled
And pink as medium-rare beef.
I dream you.

Good Old Boys Turning Over an Outhouse in South Austin, Texas, on the Night Before Halloween

It's always Beggar's Night
in the tumbledown of South Austin.

In the rear of filling stations closed
for repair, in some alley
sleek as a birth canal,
dark figures huddle to the host
of a brown bag,

their collective voices
humming like a fusebox
black with overload.

Primed, they filter talk of revival,
the unspeakable cost
of wholesale bullets, lost crops.
Again they remember in songs
strong as radiator moonshine
and their women.

When desert hawks fleck the Halloween moon
like mascara droppings,

It's time to find old-time religion
in a used car lot,
dump an outhouse,
go pissing
in the alms cup of a blind musician.

Staggering forth,
you can accept a treat of prairie wind
whipping free,
but not its penetration,
its blessed spell.

When the Hills Became West Virginia

When the wind first walked off
And whistled south,
Grass was hearsay;
Sun, the sudden rumor
Of seasons told in tongues
The sky interpreted
As a lasting impediment,
A totem of speech.

When night stood in the ground
Like a relic,
A secret keepsake
From the horizon's tomb,
A story was born
Of reeds and pine smell,
Vast spans of carnivorous green.

From one early winter to next,
A fortune in light
Wound through these hills
Like a fresh scar.
Tablets of air
Went unread.
Silence improved
Its raw reserves.

Around ice and sacred backwaters,
Among the long talks
Of trees, lectures
From rockfall, furious
Landslide omen,
Signals of other life rose
In smoke, in howls,
Somewhere beyond
This spilling thickness.

Birds here married
Midair, wings in tilt,
Under the blessing
Hands of sunshine.
And beneath oak's splitting

Bark and crook,
A braid of insects
Wormed in honor
Of nothing so beautiful,
Nothing absolute . . .

And a deer's head, dead asleep,
Educated earth
To its infinite dreaming,
Guiding small eyes upward
In terrible delight.

Then all the stones unturned
Imagined themselves
Set in a grave of mortar,
Saw nameless animals
Freeze in sight
Of new tracks.
And all stones
Spoke righteously
Of infection,
An abscess of space,
The distance narrowing
Between stone's
Word and unheard voices . . .

And in that hushed congestion,
When scents of fear
Finally lifted
In witness of cliffs,
When trails below
Burned up through evergreen
Like fuses,
The hearsay grass was crushed
Into wagon ruts, wind
Tested gingham,
Woke to the screech
Of sawmills,
Gave homespun promise
To those equipping
The dark with log fires,
Work songs, the rules
These hills would always ignore.

Southern Exposures I

All things pedestrian:

Idlers, tourists, gulls,
Bobbing late at night
Say "Viva Louisiana!"
To an agreed sight.
They move among oyster
Shells, dice throwers,
Good bones dancing
To double aces.
Straight, no chaser.
Shoptalk is lyric.
In here, iron lace
Antiques the air
And its stale roots.
The drinks I order
Disappear like prayer,
Like disappointments.
In close quarters,
I hear "Lovesick Blues"
Played on a fiddle,
The prolific dream
Of a spayed animal.
I run out of eyes.
I have no news
Of magic. No music
Flies easy from
Evening's glass
Instruments:

All things are gospel,
All unknown.

Southern Exposures II

Whenever you want to leave the clay, the deep
   furrows of your dignity, your seed
Fallen in place, you can smell cool mountain
   air in Asheville and sea bass
In Wilmington. Midnight: freight trains switch
   cars in rusting Hamlet, pass
Great silos, ponds, fields and farting sleepers
   all the way to Waycross, Ga.
A sorority of birds knows the distance, angles
   southward, runaways of love
Flocking home. What is it ahead we see dodging
   in scrub pine, in cottonwood,
In the light we dream, the nearsighted light
   of our solemn dissipations?

     *   *   *

Always the Piedmont will have its intimacies
   told in song; the stray seabird
Confused by long swells of inland foothills;
   kudzu reigning, rainfall or not.
Tobacco country: acres of white nets flutter
   in the face of Baptist restraint.
Under cattails and bladed elephant grasses,
   a marsh wind grunts hot,
Bearing the weight of morning, gray turd
   of plover, heron, red-tailed
Hawk—cousins who never meet in this life,
   this plumb beauty of stubble
We love, blowing wild-eyed, coarse, laid open
   to the hard weather of words.

Fancy Machines

"This country's tried to make our
minds fit into fancy machines."

—an unemployed auto worker

Something ordinary, whir-
ring with a valve's dark heat
in the motor pool of human

backache and combustion—
that's what we need: our own
machine to love, fit, gun

ahead in fumes, cranking alive
for one taste of fuel
and wind, your history given

to assorted rods and pistons,
a simple steering wheel,
reliable ignition, two axles

you trust implicitly.
The hard feel of the road
accelerates into your shoe,

a tit of excitement reaching
underfoot, cold nipples
of mind engaged like a clutch,

milking all you ever need
from the windshield's inner
reflection, gaining speed.

Catfishing in Natchez Trace

Some fair luck where the fickle rush of backwash
jewels. It's a sapphire day, sonnet weather,
all bordering shore and illusion. Wise fish
are guessing right at my worst hunches,
unfooled by my sinkers or choice of lure,
waving like secret flags along this river bottom
before spooling away. Again, the sporting life
unfolds expectedly: a squatting in water's sungleam,
the zigzag drift of reed beds, dead palm leaves
slapping hull, that endless roll of floorboard
between coffee breaks and quivering bait,
the circuiting spill of fuel
running engine mount to bow. Behind
rows of oleander, the sky begins rehearsing
a passing storm. Brackish water silks like whiskey.
Trolling, I switch from green-eyed flies
to doughballs and leeches, plunk this ditch of a river
with plastic bugs, until I acquire a string
of two catfish and contempt for silence . . .

It's October's music I want swarming,
the year in sudden menopause, wheeling
crosswater, over snags and wakes of browned blossoms,
down past cold stone ruins of Civil War hovels,
where families once gathered like schools
of hungry trout, mouthing nightly bible lessons
by candlelight, a ghostly reader marking his place
with a braid of fresh horsehair . . .

Listen, the boat that brought me this far knows
how the slime of fish gut greases tackle,
scaling knife, how it inhabits fiberglass and flesh.
Here, in skunk water, somewhere below channel
and open stream, miles from any legal limit,
I angle through flotsam, soft plugs of larvae,
hitting moderate chop, port tack.
Then I veer left instead of northerly
and jam fast into a mistake of a sandbar.
The propeller surges and cranks, gargles white,
whines a newborn's whine. Nothing gives. Nothing
moves, except the sun turning out in its airy socket.
Overhead, wild geese cruise this flyway,
lost for home. Coffee's gone. My compass wanders,
as if reading disheveled margins of mind.
Light bleeds light illegible in a distance
of Confederate grays. Wedged so tight, I think maybe
to dump it, swim off, abandon that bouillabaisse
of solitude, these hours nowhere,
the piddling whiskered fish I prize like manhood.
Still, pasted against a tomato sunset,
it's a manageable reality, this:
hunkered down in twilight, shanghaied
by a rocky lot of creek, snarling at the day
that closes like a chilled pore, my shadow
now darting in a reel of backroad Mississippi;
and me, telling stories of men
to relieved, understanding bullheads.

Sequels to an Uncollected Winter

1. *Morning of Crystal*

This is the deathless body, and this
the land's blood . . . and here the wine-laced sky
over Iowa resembles a heavenly parfait.
In one more day Des Moines
will be diapered by first snow. A young girl,
barely real, glazes the sidewalk
with a stupid look. Iowa in winter always
dumbfounds the love in us.
Before long, nothing opposes the weight and resolution
of this sky, this wilderness of earth
hardening. When heaviness strikes like a clock
glowing incandescently, the season
opens to itself, as if a familiar stunt
in a traveling show, a fabulation only
a touched young girl can devise for any new world.

Des Moines. November 1973

2. *Cooking the Cold*

In our smoke house,
in hot fog of hickory and buckeye chips,
we hang meats

like vignettes, independent
of all but the bones
we crack

and soup. Outside,
it's the same white shimmering
Ohio country

we trust like an open palm,
like an apothecary.
And in these crosswinds,

as our fire builds,
stirrings of primordial dusk begin
fogging in.

Shelby County, Ohio. December 1974

3. *Ice Finesse*

Long Christmas evening in a farm woman's bed,
I warm like a quilt.
A December of junctions,
dark, unlittered, airy as entry
into fable, cutting against grains
of propriety. We are decent
enough, naked in the self-paintings
we brush like hair. On holy night,
waking to the screech of pipes bursting
in winter's elaborate dwelling,
our spines ice us
upright, like posts in the sheets.
Assured of disaster,
we fall back to swarm over
the gifts
from our polished skins.

Independence, Missouri. December 1975

4. *The Certainties*

Kept animals stray in the wind-driven snow twenty miles
    northwest
Out of Minneapolis, white-faced heifers each searching
    the eyes
Of the others, doomed. These distances blowing closed
    over roads
And county fences, emanate from the hardest parts of us
    like certainties.
At desolate junctures, hardly moving, a gunshot of breath
    signals
The residue of soul. On this barren, narrow towpath,
    the hung
Bellies of cows lunge through drifts forming whale tracks,
    inching
Ahead, the beasts hopeful as drifters at the hiring gate.
    Night-hammered,
Blizzard-ripe, we wait by the window with house plants,
    our fears
Nearly realized, a salt lick of faith turning to stone
    in our bowels.

Coon Rapids, Minnesota. January 1976

5. *An Undoing*

My horses are dead,
but the hail has gone.

Three hundred miles south
the ground is fit to plant.

I rinse out in a wind,
dreaming of lumber.

Logs and dead crops
appear in my songs.

In this looseleaf country,
I can bury and build.

Rightly, it is winter.
I won't need more horses.

Shelby County, Indiana. February 1977

6. *On the Upside*

On Hubbard Street, among factory signs
And the gay bars further west, this winter
In the ditch does not mean enough.
With innocence, a melodrama of duty
Is played by the big Pole city workers,
Flinging rock salt, unplugging sewers
In defense of a surprise freeze.
Their smiles, like habits, break hard.
Their black stocking caps appear
Stark and vulnerable to the young men cruising
Past hand-in-hand, swimming at noon
Toward darkened theaters and bargain hotels,
Requiring sweet ambush, a ration
Of luxury. These filthy buildings don't care,
Can't whistle insults. Soon the Poles,
Immutable as mud, will have picked
These streets clean of ice
And loitering glances, will filter
Home to dinners of wurst and bock beer,
Laying odds against more snow.
And slowly, in its timeliness, a clothesline
Of color will string through the city,
Flapping proudly, ready for collision
With high blue skies, like old lovers
Tossing again in a warehouse loft, straining free.

Northside Chicago. March 1978

Part Three

Killing Time

Shopping for Midnight

There you go, it's everywhere
here, waiting for me at ridiculous prices,
   the essential mood—collected
and perfect-bound—hidden, certainly,
      like the best of bargains,
among tampons & pickles & paperwares,
   down these aisles I tour at midnight.

A browser at heart,
I carry no money. It's safer that way,
   as the average retail clerk
will ply me with replicas, expensive
      imitations of my prize.
And I have been taken for an easy target
   before, buying dreams of blood

and summer at discount.
Once, guilty of wearing an oversized coat
   to market, a thief, I resisted
the sweet commerce of a career angel,
      boosting her instead
of her temporary goods. But shopping
   for the darkest of bones demands nerve,

a special setting, instinct.
There are, naturally, no rules of search
   or purchase; no adequate samples.
Not necessary. The time will arrive when
      I round a corner perfectly
and find it, waiting like a mouse, enormous
   as Canada, the perennial top-shelf item.

It belongs somewhere, and only
there, mine to find alone, marked down
   like contaminated vegetables,
a fish found breathing on the beach, harvest
      of any old night, dampish,
twisted, leaving me to decide whether
   to steal, borrow, or merely adore it.

Oyster Love

Oystermen claim they can easily tell the sex
of oysters and insist that females should be
fried and males should be stewed.

—Joy of Cooking

I sense them below southern waters,
Sweet plugs of sputum
Whirling in a journey of gray silence.

I am backed only by lights of towns
I drift past absently,
Circling overnight, one with the air.

Measure by measure, this watching
Turns to lines
Running twelve arms deep, crossing

And not crossing. I let more drop.
The water holds.
I bend like a knuckle, gathering

Net. In this bay there are calls
From obstinate things:
Extinct whispers, a creaking of ropes.

I'd do better to translate the mouth
Of a fog or sad current
That dwindles to a final, terse shiver

Along this coast. I sing a little;
I know the song
Of wet acres gleaming by nightshine.

I work some hole in midnight's water,
Heaving my catch back
On board—rocks for stew and frying,

Alive as stars. I consider the vague
Sex of my game idly:
Pile after pile, their gummy lips

Driven apart by irritations of sand
And pleasure, open
To squalls of love on the bottom.

All pressure's topside, a barometer
Of time closing me
Down, dead center in another dawn.

I yawn for home, leathery, coloring
Like a new bruise,
Stretching toward shore and bedrock.

Darkly, in periodic sun, I slash
The muscles of night
Free, and suck raw from half shells.

Drinking Beer

There was this woman selling
Orchids from a shore of the Amazon.
She had nothing to do
With the white beginning

To stray from her fluttering hands
Like porcelain birds,
Or the fact, across this earth,
East of Pittsburgh,

Only one place
In the harbor district
Throbs like an untrussed hernia
And permits dancing Sunday nights.

Regulars crash and stick here
As if the aimless work
Of an apprentice knife thrower.
I hang here, too,

Watering the gaunt mule of my life.
Outside, the sun dives
Wherever it dives, while I toast
A glass to one man's family in a wallet.

Behind the bar, jars of sausage
And pickled eggs stare back
Like the dismantled organs
Of a space traveler.

I study a 1910 ferrotype
Of John L. Sullivan, countryman—
His hands wrapped like baked potatoes;
His dumb face swollen with dreams.

I examine backroads of my knuckles,
Visit the men's room twice.
I stack loose change
And treat the house to a favorite

Jukebox fever. Somebody belches
A ball score. Someone
Sighs. We are all counting
On the bottom of the ninth,

Or one wink from that lady dozing
In the far corner booth,
Who sails the orchid waters
Of her drunk, a porcelain bird.

Eargasms

(Unscheduled flights to the Inner Household)

Many bush pilots flying blind
through the dark canals of our ears;
sometimes they parachute
into fields of skull fur,
survive, build huts, raise families.

Wintering in a Dream by Van Gogh

A winter of avocados
and pillowed genuflections,

long crabwalks into the sun's pavilion.
These chalk-yellow beaches
bleed at Christmas, feel
muscular, unofficially famous,
half-drawn to calm
by rehearsed stigmata.

I jog through the crimson window of a heart,
a familiar organ or my left ventricle:
some cardiovascular song
picnicking alone

in the holiday weather of one painter's waste . . .
No one here tans or drowns. No one gawks
at an ear's happy death. Harmonics of light

shift as sawdust in tourist winds.
In the crystal clearing of January mornings,
I decorate this tropical escape
with castle sewage and music from lagoons,
defining all pigment

as the rainbow feet of art's precious thief.

Turning Thirty

Soon you will remove your last black boot
To go barefooted, and blind to boot,

Your hot tracks vanishing in a late rain
Like taxis. Still, you select the rain,

Expecting miracles, prescribing a dance
Which can't be interpreted as dance

Alone. The old propoganda of clouds
Is helpful, too, when entering clouds

Of forgetfulness like a grappling hook.
Then you get lucky, break a leg, hook

Onto the level life you skunked all year.
Twenty-nine, naturally, was a fine year

For crashes: Try a dive into the familiar
Spaces of your skull, or unfamiliar

Doorways like a drunk in foggy orbit,
Even houses of skin, forever at orbit.

In barefeet, you greet the feel of water.
To the sky above, you are only water.

Forgive the sky its clutter, your body
Slumped in this park, an accidental body.

The park delivers the camouflage you love,
That obscurity, a simple menu of love

Offered as footnote to the wild fiction
Told to the heart at midnight: A fiction

Of surfaces and fingerprints, the story
Of the blind astronomer, all within a story.

In a flush of dreams dealt like poker hands,
You sing sightless, talking with your hands

Full of pencils, a tin cup of air.
None of your bones rust without an air

Of madness. Soon you must flee your changes.
Soon you can maneuver by the braille of changes.

Words for a Dissolving Morning

I smell like milk. So what? The Czechs
Are out buying wine and pistols for lunch.
Observe: defenses of their hearts, their fists.
I am still thinking of myself and milk,
The willow I crushed in Rhode Island's fall,
An answer for my gaping freedoms.
I cannot speak as clearly as my shirt
Or the skinny legs of Puerto Ricans.
A day breaks, trails off like a strand
Of dental floss. I imagine I know
How real teeth grow around opinions
And charity. I don't. I have lamb chops
To bread, lemons to peel, a country
Sprawling between its bones and sagging chin.
The fists on my door shatter like fine china.

Love Poem: Poison

I am a poison
inside of you.
Some raw pork.

A black orchid.

I fit below
your belt
like a cold
jelly, and wait . . .

There is a pulse
inside of you.
A mouth and breast.

A steel onion.

I borrow your parts
like a neighbor.
Sugar, ice, lard:
a pack rat's store.
I need your throat
to finish it . . .

to work my way
into the nail
of your brain
like a bubble
of air . . .
and it's over.

An orchid in ice.
A bad meal.

I am a poison.
I am a poison

inside of you.
A long winter
out of work.

Love Poem: Time Fuses

I am the cunning hand grenade.
I dangle in your head
like a plumb.

A contraption of bolts and wax,
I bob like a sea mine
in your sugarcane blood,
that sewer of champagne.

Surely shrapnel is lighter than love.

New Liniments

All night my hair whirs graciously.
It speaks like an old athlete
Praising the fixed games of heaven.

There is no suitable explanation
For the sad arithmetic of days.
My hair, like a shot-putter's sleep,

Hits with a dreamless, empty thud.
It walks handcuffed to the ecstasy
I wear in the fashionable dark.

Each night a territory blossoms,
Supple and hard as a blackjack.
My hair raids the silence of it.

My hair accepts the threat of rain
And windy evenings, always dying,
Like ivy, from the roots up.

Gradually, the liquid night grows
Older, into morning and pine breeze.
Eyelids snap alive; sperm cells drone.

My hair stands cocked like a boxer.
My hair will hold its own among
The lethal new liniments of love.

Brothers

I

Let a shark guard
The shores of your body.
His patrol is a mile of stars . . .

II

We can dream sharks
In the shallow bars of this lake,
Chewing sour legs and echoes.
We keep away
The shadows that nudge our oar
With their dark sides.
Drawn by the bloods we share,
They hang on like sleep
In this, a water season.

III

The lake still prospers.
Mechanics dredge its bottom for parts
And skim oil off in pails.
I drag for your body.
I find the moon
In my net, a withered fin.
I pull a fist of water back.
I find a cellophane bag.
There is a map
Of daylight, a photograph, too.
This is your return.

IV

We wake in cold water.
There are children
A mile below us, twinkling
Like the eyes of chimps in jars . . .
We dissolve from their light
Together, under stars,
In the noose of the lake.

Caitlin's Poem

—for my daughter

Lifting now to voices,
shifting shapes, tendrils
of air, you join

an essay of people.
You join, and renew again,
old women from Dingle,

Kerry, washboard America—
your provincial mothers
wrapped like skirts,

bundled under earth,
each fertilizing a time.
Some begged for drink,

laughter, for a kindness,
all reciting poetics
of kitchen, street, church.

They direct you somehow,
their ancient ways sweeping
through new blood—

your soft, sweet edges,
your first body
wrinkled like a peach stone.

There is this haystack
of eyes, daughter,
the menace of affection

told in visits,
gravy kisses, gifts
of silver and wood block.

Kate, beware and rejoice
in the same breath,
but don't hold it too long.

Wear us like a raincoat,
my love, then shed us
in a flush of sunlight.

We'll call it love,
call it order, our hearts.
Consider mechanics,

law, a life in medicine,
the everlasting fix
of your mother's fine face.

Baby, woman—it snows.
We are ignorant
of snow, its perfect

lurking promise. No matter.
We're snow beings,
ice dolls, figures of mind,

ripe for sunstroke.
Far off, wild as lightning
and marshgrass,

you will own all your own
blind possibilities.
No brooding ever helps

sell fatherly strategies—
save little things,
like you, or a blessing

of weeds, wind that tunes
us like pianos,
a legacy of blood's wine

and vinegar. It's this,
babe: a haul of high waters,
with or without oars.

Michael's Poem

—for my son

In this scrawl of time and instance
of wind insisting breath
in you and you with us—
a textured, blueing presence

silky and gleaming like a snub revolver
or vintage crystal. On balance,
you prove routinely original:
heir to a casino of years,

the hard knuckle, a miner's awkward
embrace. Lost to clearings
by the sea, North Country haze
of pine light, we offer thanks

and password. Among edges,
the twines of loose fitting sheets,
we can move and preserve.
Michael, all manner

of palette and absence,
faint music, ahead:
after memory,
praise; before reflection,

task. And then always, again,
the lean shiver
of protocol abandoned
for one clue to winter's repeated sky.

Rat Hunting

Draining pea soup from a thermos mug
One August, my grandfather, heroless
And taut in the clear level air
Off Lake Erie, haunches
Over a plan, his land, and me.

His finger stirs a strategy
In dirt, circling urgent points
Of attack: "Here and maybe here,"
He indirects, barely remembering
The black behind our cellar door,
The horrible, toothy intruders
Who rule his rust garden of tools
And unmended lawn chairs.
He revises some, and trims a bit
To account for youthful sloppiness.
We have an understanding
About backpedaling on the job
Or asking questions: We do neither.
Now I see him rise from the woods,
Club in hand, across the stray grass
Sticking through clay like hairs
In the landscape of an old man's nose.
Now striding toward the crawl space,
Now telling me, "You'll help."
              *   *   *
So I follow him in,
Watching the bush
Arena of August
Turn jungle
Wild. Sparrows
Observe our
Mission's march
Like Great Lakes
Buzzards. White fire
Of prehistoric dust
Welcomes our entry.

In the dark, things
Multiply. In the dark,
We get even.
He sweats into a grin.
He thumbs his weapon
With affection. Air
Sits in my chest
Like a scalpel.
I breathe in,
And hold it.

Then he strikes
The floor
Pounds the
Fur scenery
Shotguns
The earth
Red.

    *   *   *

When you finished we hung
Windless as touchdown passes,
Done with our record catch
Before dinner. Head turned
Away, I carried a fistful
Of tails, curling like worms,
To a creek, being helpful.
Grandfather, August's here
Again. It's double martinis
In the midwest now, ten years
Since hunting quit you for good.
And gin itself can't cool the air
Or rid my land of vermin.
Tonight I wanted us on paper,
Breathing in these poor lines
Once more, burning like weeds
Under panes of glass, knowing
All I keep strikes me right:
My same name and nervous mouth,
And you, old battler,
Stirring in my blood like a rat.

Part Four

Repairs

Cycle for Claes Oldenburg

1. *Hard Scissors*

Starting out as steel
it snips a path

from Sweden
to unreal Chicago.

This handsome
cargo edges

homeward,
case-hardened,

a guardian of customs.
It threatens

inwardly.
Eyes

forward:
the great sheers

arrive
unharmed by

Swedish love,
American law.

2. *Soft Scissors*

These limp fingers whip
  a perfect curve,
    cutting
  across the eye
    like paper.

There is so little chance
  for even the finest
    bond.

3. *Saws*

SAWS PROTECT US.
ART WON'T.
SAWS CHEW THE MEAT
ART LAYS AT OUR FEET.
WHEN THE SAWS FINISH,
A STILLNESS CUTS HOME.

4. *Knees*

It is small music
played between knees.
The foot's gone,
the thigh dissolved
like powdered milk.
Knees quiver
a cappella.
They stay young,
supple and numb.
Above each one,
legs far away,
the air clots
in rare celebration.

5. *John Kennedy Underground*

At the elegant inaugural of time,
The spirit thins quickly
Into the richest of all sleeps.
Underground, he turns down
For keeps. He wears this death
Like the tuxedo it is,
Lying at the bottom
Of forever's morning after.

We stare like guns.
We want him back
Triggering
National heartbreak.

In a democracy of soil,
Only the bushwhacked caucus.
No cabinet clamors angry
Here, no flags of distress.
In art, we must let
The object resume its death.

6. *Plugs*

In love,
the plugs
object to
any foreplay
the outlet
requires.

Pronged,
the entry
is grand,
yet failing
voltage,
quite useless.

7. *The Punching Bag Tombstone*

Winter buries things
Heavy with winter, Claes.
But you breeze
Into the season's ambush
With transfixing logic:
Yes, and again, no.
Those beaten triumph.
The boxers of snow
Press jabs against
Your cunning monument.
No use, the uppercut fixes
Fame like a star.
I say your grave
Has integrity. You fit.

When You Witness a Deer

1. When you witness a deer being eaten over by packs
   of happy dogs, act like a poem. Move closer to the
   carcass. Examine its one black eye for alliterative
   possibilities, observing metaphors on the partly
   chewed tongue. Now taste what the dogs have left.

2. As a poem you will want to study traits of the
   assassin, convict and priest. Be fitted for their
   singular robes. Then take a job disguised as an
   insurance salesman.

3. Or, accept a position in a prosthetics warehouse.
   Take stock of things along the shelves according to
   your understanding of replacement parts and human
   tentacles.

4. If you become lonelier than a turtle, dance the
   mazurka of ungodly dreams. Find a gypsy; steal his
   special herbs and bury them in an East Texas
   swamp. You can sleep between he and his wife like
   a rattle in the hand of their stillborn child.

5. Each day accept a shortness of breath for what it
   is. Ignite sunsets. Dwell in selected mine shafts.
   Kick the teeth out from mandatory smiles.

6. Later on, travel to a local orphanage and foster an insurrection. Chanting the code of burglars, steal in among the naked children to shave their heads with a usable cliche. This corruption must be your answer to soft-spoken eulogies.

7. Speak like a ball. Or develop your own alphabet. God will still be sailing his dinghy in the bloodstream of ants.

8. At first hint of rejection, rent a flat in Brooklyn. Furnish it with lemon trees and quill pens and gallons of dried saliva. Now mail yourself to any post office in San Francisco to wait among the faces of wanted criminals.

9. Reject revisions; resist translation. Say nothing more than that which is understood by animals who hunt their young.

10. Dogs have picked up the scent of your stunning couplets, so the drama is almost complete. Read yourself again in final version from the pages of a popular gardening manual. Then quick, dissolve from memory like a wartime loan.

The Dance of the Place Itself

I

Crossing Beacon Hill like a jar of melodies,
A man playing hopscotch
On the last legs of the sun.
He leaps ahead, a wallpaper angel
With torpedoes up his sleeve,
Aiming at those who want to play
And those who won't go home.
He pencils himself into my notes:
"Something sudden as gypsy wolves
Leaving at dawn in a boxcar of bribes."

II

Today I lean my crowbar
on the eternal etceteras,
a filibuster of dreams . . .

Days drift out like barges
with a cargo of fingertips.
I burn in my morning sleep.

III

At noon another piped-in dream
Unravels as music at the far end of a field,
Through hospital wards like a white cord,
In among patients who are getting fat dancing
In tandem, on the balls of their feet.

What can challenge these nightly blindfolds?
What swings to the rhythms of my street on a beard?
It's Beacon Hill snatching a place in its dance.

IV

I attend my sleep
in some other skin,
an animal's nightshirt.
Cobblestones in love
with my face lie
silent as clowns
at a midnight eviction.
Allegro or jingle,
I don't know song
from airshafts
anymore. I simply
wake and stare
at planks of shade,
intense as plywood.

V

Goodbye Heaven, imagination fails you.
Here I play croquet in wet sneakers.
And my words grow thicker with use,
The chunky arms of a wheelchair rider.

Astronauts in Love

*   *   *

Perhaps you have heard
how we are powered
high within an eye's
final probings of indigo,

heads and spirits above
a planet gone lean
on heroes and windfall.

When hurled to the decorous dark
we are what you desire:

a gesture propelled
genius unassembled
courage of young gods
newly entombed.

Yes, we cleanse the ionosphere
like brookwater—

first up, then splashing down

*   *   *

Women especially
love us, at least love
our technical mysteries.
It's all equilibrium,
a balanced dance
to the celestial music
of stars collapsing.
Love is full of such
queer concussions

*   *   *

To be a dark particle, sweet
catalog of echoes.
In the custody of starshine,

we are official
as asterisks,
sequential achievements
in the future's news

*　*　*

Eh, but tonight, north of anywhere,
behaving microscopic,
we navigate the solitary harbors
of minor moons, tethered by chords

and taut rationale. Out here,
when we think to touch
ourselves thinning
into model theorems,
we slide inside
nylon sleeves, prevail
as strategic risks,
debris of oaths
expelled in false orbit

*　*　*

Regarding our wiggles
on the hook of space:

we persist
without weather

or footfall,
occupiable season

or mindful tug
from love's gravity.

In positive alignment
with strangers here,

we lack research
into propositions

of goodwill
among beings,

of being
gulped whole

    *   *   *

All year at space
knowing the hour and precise
digital sweep of instrumentation,
awash in tracings
of habitat,

we proceed by designs
of double-talk,
delusions of repair,
breeding us cold and neuter
as eels

    *   *   *

Adrift in morning exercise
and prayer, turning other ways,
too, as if preserved
as what remains
of ivory-shadowed patterns
trembling on the interior hull
like eyelids.

So it continues static the question
how to hollow our cold cores,
answer the ellipsis . . .how
to court magnificence
reflected within our visors

    *   *   *

Ghosts at the astral window float
immense, circumspect, fleeting
as children drifting silent
with a sexual grace.

No real elegance in wings,
only haphazard memory
of shreds and strands,

exposure to green images,
sudden illuminations of landshed